RAPTORS
OWLS

JULIE K. LUNDGREN

ROURKE
PUBLISHING
Vero Beach, Florida 32964

www.rourkepublishing.com

Project Assistance:
The author also thanks raptor specialist Frank Taylor and the team at Blue Door Publishing.

Photo credits: Cover © Konstantin Tavrov; Title Page © Brooke Whatnall; Contents Page © Ecoprint; Page 4 © Terry L. Sohl; Page 5 © Gertjan Hooijer; Page 7 © Jill Lang; Page 8 © Daniel Hebert; Page 9 © Eric Isselée; Page 10 © Henk Bentlage; Page 11 © Dennis Donohue; Page 12 © Dr. Morley Read; Page 13 © dragon_fang; Page 14 © Jill Lang; Page 15 © Michael Woodruff; Page 16 © FloridaStock; Page 17 © Norman Bateman; Page 18 © Marilyn Barbone; Page 19 © Paul S. Wolf; Page 20 © Timothy Large; Page 21 © Elemental Imaging; Page 22 © Stephen Coburn.

Editor: Meg Greve

Cover and page design by Nicola Stratford, Blue Door Publishing

Library of Congress Cataloging-in-Publication Data

Lundgren, Julie K.
  Owls / Julie K. Lundgren.
      p. cm. -- (Raptors)
  Includes index.
  ISBN 978-1-60694-395-3 (hard cover)
  ISBN 978-1-60694-773-9 (soft cover)
  1. Owls--Juvenile literature. I. Title.
  QL696.S83L86 2010
  598.9'7--dc22
                                        2009000528

Rourke Publishing
Printed in the United States of America, North Mankato, Minnesota
102010
102010LP-A

www.rourkepublishing.com - rourke@rourkepublishing.com
Post Office Box 643328 Vero Beach, Florida 32964

Contents

A WORLD OF OWLS

Owls live in deserts, forests, grasslands, and the cold, northern plains. They can be found on all continents except Antarctica. Like other **raptors**, owls hunt animals for food. They come in many sizes.

An adult elf owl weighs about the same as a spoon. It captures spiders, scorpions, and large insects for food.

4

The Eurasian eagle owl is the world's largest kind of owl. They stand 23 to 28 inches (58 to 71 centimeters) tall.

Owl feathers have soft edges for silent flight. The colors of the feathers help them blend in with their surroundings like natural **camouflage**, allowing them to escape the notice of enemies like **goshawks**, crows, house cats, and other owls. Feathers cover owls from head to toe.

More than 160 kinds of owls live in the world, including 19 in North America.

North America

Europe

Asia

Africa

South America

Australia

RAPTOR REPORT

Eastern screech owls live in the forest. Their feathers look like tree bark.

7

Snowy owls are one of the few kinds of owls that hunt during the day. Other daytime hunters include burrowing owls and short-eared owls.

FEATHERED TIGERS

Owls have four toes per foot. Each toe ends with a sharp **talon**. Two toes always point forward and one always points back. Like a human thumb, the fourth toe can move either forward or back, to help the owl grip **prey**. Owls also have strong, hooked beaks for tearing meat into small bites.

9

Big eyes help **nocturnal** owls hunt in the dark. Like human eyes, owl eyes face forward, allowing them to judge distance. Owl ears are slits hidden behind their face feathers. Their flat faces collect sound and direct it to their ears.

Because owls cannot roll or turn their eyes, they turn their heads to see in different directions. Owls can turn their heads to see directly behind them.

RAPTOR REPORT

IMPORTANT

Great grey owls can hear mice tunneling under deep snow. They use their powerful legs and feet to reach through and grab them.

Owls often swallow **prey** whole. Whatever they cannot digest, like bones, fur, and feathers, they spit up as an owl **pellet**. Wildlife scientists and others curious about nature collect and take apart the pellets to discover what the owls have been eating.

Look for owl pellets at the base of tree trunks. If you find one, carefully pull it apart. Fur and little skulls with teeth mean a rodent, while feathers and skulls without teeth mean a bird. Wash your hands well when you finish your investigation.

skull with teeth

fur

claw

RAPTOR REPORT

IMPORTANT

IMPORTANT

Owls often carry their prey to a nearby perch, where they can hide and eat in peace.

"Whoo, whoo, who cooks for you?", the barred owl seems to say. Bird watchers make up words for the hoots of different owls to help them remember their calls.

Owl Talk

Different kinds of owls have different kinds of calls. They screech, whistle, bark, hiss, and, of course, hoot. Owls commonly hoot to claim and defend their **territory**. In late winter and early spring, they call to find a mate.

Each spring, male Northern saw-whet owls repeat short toots to attract a female, sometimes for hours.

NESTS AND OWLETS

Owls nest in different places depending on where they live. Forest owls may live in holes in trees or open nests high in the branches. Most owls take over the old nests of other animals instead of building their own.

This young great-horned owl stretches its wings on a nest made of sticks.

Burrowing owls live in grasslands and nest underground, often in old prairie dog tunnels.

An owl female lays eggs in the nest and keeps them warm. The male brings her food. After the eggs hatch, the female sits over the owlets until they have enough body fat to keep themselves warm.

Owlets make their wings stronger for flying by hopping and flapping from branch to branch. Sometimes they fall from the tree. They are usually unhurt, and their parents continue to protect and feed them.

RAPTOR REPORT

★ IMPORTANT ★

Great-horned owl parents will deliver meals to their hungry young for several months, until they learn to catch their own.

 OWL MAGIC

Owls face many dangers caused by people. They may be shot, hit by cars, accidently poisoned by pesticides, or driven from their territories by tree cutting or construction. Learning about owls and their needs is the first step in helping them.

Many wildlife organizations offer building plans for owl nest boxes. Screech owls, saw-whet owls, and barn owls happily move in.

RAPTOR REPORT

People must balance the need for cutting trees for lumber, paper, and other products with the needs of the animals that make their homes in the forest.

On a moonlit night, go owling! Take a walk in a park, nature area, or woodsy neighborhood. Owls often answer other owls they hear calling. Try an owl hoot and listen carefully. It may reveal the magical world of owls.

LOSSARY

camouflage (KAM-uh-flahzh): coloring or shape that allows an animal to blend in with its surroundings

goshawks (GAHS-hawks): a kind of large forest raptor that eats other birds

nocturnal (nock-TER-nuhl): active at night

pellet (PEHL-iht): a small, wet mass of bones, fur, feathers, and other prey parts coughed up by raptors after eating

prey (PRAY): animals that are hunted and eaten by other animals

raptors (RAP-terz): birds that use their sharp beaks and feet to eat other animals, including hawks, eagles, falcons, and owls

talon (TAL-uhn): a raptor's sharp claw

territory (TAIR-uh-tor-ee): the area of land that an animal will defend as its own

Index

Websites to Visit

Soar over to your local library to learn more about owls and other raptors. Hunt down the following websites:

www.hawkandowl.org

www.hawkwatch.org/home/

www.kidwings.com/index.htm

www.owling.com/

www.owlpages.com

About The Author

Julie K. Lundgren grew up near Lake Superior where she reveled in mucking about in the woods, picking berries, and expanding her rock collection. Her interest in nature led her to a degree in biology and eight years of volunteer work at The Raptor Center at the University of Minnesota. She currently lives in Minnesota with her husband and two sons.